LEAVE WORK EARLY AND GO TO THE BAR

SURPRISING MANAGEMENT SECRETS TO
CREATE HIGHLY PRODUCTIVE TEAMS IN ANY
BUSINESS

BRUCE WOLF

WOLF MOUNTAIN
– PUBLISHING –

ISBN 978-1-952286-07-0 (paperback)

ISBN 978-1-952286-06-3 (ebook)

Dedicated to my beautiful wife for giving me some time to write this (and for going to the bar with me).

CONTENTS

FOREWORD

I'm from Wisconsin.

We go to bars.

I'm not talking about the smoke-filled corner bars with ripped felt on the pool table and one tiny window with a neon sign and a metal grate. I'm talking about the nicer bars, places with big windows and leather sofas, places where the wine list is longer than the beer tap and none of the bartenders have trucker hats or mullets.

They're great places to hang out and talk with coworkers, but I understand they aren't for everyone.

If they aren't for you or your teammates, go to a coffee shop instead. If you don't care for coffee shops, go to a bakery. Got a problem with bakeries? Try a mall food court, a corner diner, or one of those trendy hipster places with free wifi where everyone wears air pods and writes poetry.

Just find a place to go that isn't your regular office space.

You don't go to the office to connect with your friends, do you?

If you do, maybe this isn't the book for you - you can put it back on the shelf or hit the back button on your browser right now and save us both a lot of trouble.

Most people don't call their friends on a Friday night and say "Yeah, let's all meet the office and hang out!" If you wanna connect with people and build real, meaningful relationships, your office is a terrible place to do it.

Having a highly productive team requires people to have connected relationships. It's not the only thing, but it's definitely one of the most important things.

Going to a bar (or a bakery or a hipster tearoom) isn't always looked at as the best way to foster a highly productive team, but I'll wager a lot of the people who grumble at the mention of leaving work early to go to the bar once in a while don't have highly productive teams.

This book looks at the methods and practices that rank-and-file sheep-herding managers don't take the time to examine - the methods and practices that create teams that are not only highly productive, but actually full of happy people!

Being happy and being productive, as so damn few managers seem to realize, actually tend to go hand in hand.

I've worked for all sorts of companies over the course of my career (Fortune 100, Private 100, global niche leader, franchisee, regional chain, small companies, dot com startups, secular organizations, volunteer organizations, nonprofits, educational institutions, sole proprietorships) and consulted with leaders from many more.

Over time, I noticed some things.

One thing I noticed is that every organization - no matter how big or small, no matter what industry or location - emphasizes teamwork. They all want highly productive teams, and they all want the amazing momentum and productivity that comes from a group of people that work well together.

I've also noticed that no matter the size of a company, where they're located, or what industry they're in, their leaders make the same productivity-killing mistakes over and over. There are poor habits subconsciously ingrained in business culture.

This book is gonna kick the doors in on the worst of those issues, expose the root causes, and show you how to avoid them.

So let's dive into understanding the mistakes leaders make when they try to put together a highly productive team and learn how to do better!

PART I

BUILDING A HIGHLY PRODUCTIVE TEAM

1

WHAT DO YOU WANT?

I f you want a highly productive team, the first thing you're going to have to do is... wait for it... build a team.

Don't make it complicated, though - a team is just a group of people with a common goal.

It doesn't matter if it's at an old-money Fortune 50 enterprise, a hot new startup, or a bowling team, it's just a group of people working together towards a common goal.

This idea seems so simple, but we have a tendency to forget it when we get into the details of fostering a highly productive team, beginning with the first step.

This first step might also be the most important step. Getting the wrong person on a team is one of the biggest problems a manager can have. Not only will having the wrong person hamper productivity, it's not an easy fix, and (as we'll discuss more later) it can impact the productivity of the rest of your team, too.

So if we're building a team, we should "begin with the end in mind," like Stephen Covey says. I think most organizations get this part right.

Ask any leader what kind of people they want on their team, and they'll pretty much always say things like:

- "I want someone who works well with others."
- "I want someone who's motivated and driven."
- "I want someone who's engaged, someone who cares about doing a great job."

These are pretty much universal traits that every leader wants in the people on their team (I mean, nobody wants a guy who pisses everyone off and doesn't care if work gets done, right?).

There's a good reason everyone says they want these traits in their teammates: they're critical to highly productive teams.

It would be logical for managers to look for these traits at every step of the process, then, right?

Of course it would.

But do people handle building a team (which might be the most critical part of their job) logically?

Let's go deeper and find out.

2

PEOPLE REVIEW RESUMES LIKE IDIOTS

Ok, we know that a team is just a group of people and we know that we want people who work well with others, are motivated and driven, and care about doing a great job.

So when a typical manager puts out a job posting and starts looking at resumes, what do they look for?

Education and most recent job title.

Now you're probably thinking yourself, "Well that doesn't make any sense."

You're damn right it doesn't!

Yet it happens, unfailingly, in nearly every hiring situation for every job everywhere.

The challenge first comes up when resumes start dropping into our inbox and we look for those qualities.

Dig deep into the resumes you received for your last posting. Do you see anyone that says they work well with others, are highly motivated, and care about doing a great job?

It happens, but odds are pretty high that those qualities aren't on there.

So why doesn't everyone put that stuff on their resumes?

Because we know how resumes are consumed. There's plenty of articles on key-word theories and hiring psychology, and they condition us to write our resumes in a very specific and prescribed way.

The first step your resume has to get through is some jackass Applicant Tracking System (ATS for those who know the HR biz). These wonderful time-saving software tools can't tell the difference between "MBA" and "M.B.A." but they decide which candidates a hiring manager gets to look at.

On the off chance a resume happens to make it through the robot review (which cares far more about precisely formatted keywords than building a highly productive team), the hiring managers and HR reviewers get it next. They scan the resume and look for two things:

- Education
- Most Recent Job Title

That's it.

Most leaders skim through all those carefully crafted phrases and painstakingly inserted keywords to just glance at two mundane pieces of information to make their initial assessment.

Oh, but not you, I'm sure. You're a better manager than that.

I'll bet you pore over every detail of every damn

resume that crosses your inbox, meticulously researching for hidden clues in every phrase that will let you know if this person has what you're really looking for.

Sure, ok, but no one else does that. Here's proof:

ImpactHiringSolutions.com says recruiters only look at a resume for 20 seconds "many days I have reviewed hundreds of resumes and most in less than 20 seconds" (http://www.impacthiringsolutions.com/careerblog/2010/01/18/how-recruiters-read-resumes-in-10-seconds-or-less/).

FastCompany.com doesn't even get that deep into resume reviews - they say the average is only 7.4 seconds (https://www.fastcompany.com/90263970/your-resume-only-gets-7-4-seconds-to-make-an-impression-heres-how-to-stand-out).

Forbes, a longtime stalwart of peak business practices, says each resume only gets glanced at for 5 seconds (https://www.forbes.com/sites/jackkelly/2018/05/15/your-resume-has-only-five-seconds-to-grab-someones-attention-here-is-what-you-should-do-now/#5382e20c6d22).

In each of these cases, and in countless other articles, studies, and interviews, the same message is repeated over and over again: education and most recent job title are the only two things that get looked at when someone looks at a resume for the first time.

Resume reviewers say they don't have enough time to review the multitude of resumes that come in to any level of depth.

Big mistake.

Sure, there's lots of ways to justify this approach and

when I talk to hiring managers about it, the two answers I hear most often are:

- I have too much to do
- If they can't write a good resume, they're not a good enough communicator

That first one?

That's completely on you.

You don't have time? I can't help you there. If you don't have time to put any extra effort into finding the best candidates to join your team, this book won't help you a lick.

No book will.

Sure, you can throw your money away at some sunshine-shooting author that'll tell you they have the magic step that no one else knows to find the perfect candidate in no time at all. You might even find a rep from some people-centric startup that'll convince you they've cracked the code to join lost wisdom of the ancients with mind-blowing 30th century algorithms to bring you a resume scanner guaranteed to find the number one leader in whatever pile of garbage resumes you can jam into it.

But that ain't me.

That's not what this book is about.

I've seen those things.

I've seen the results.

More of the same.

More cranking people through the funnel. More teams full of 'meh' candidates going through the motions.

More status meetings where everyone is staring at each other trying to remember what they were talking about.

You can have that.

Chuck this book in the trash and go find the email address for that slick sales guy with the nice teeth from SuperAmazingResumeGenie.com. Good luck.

If you want a highly productive team, you're actually gonna have to do some work. It's going to take some time.

The good news is that putting in the time is half the battle at this step.

As for the second excuse (If they can't write a good enough resume, they must not be a good communicator), that just sounds like a cop-out.

First off, unless it's a communications position, that shouldn't be their strong suit. Yes, everyone needs to communicate, but how often are you going to ask them to communicate the type of information you're looking for in a resume?

And are *you* a good communicator?

What does your job description look like?

I don't know about you, but when I look at a random job description, I'd say on average somewhere between 85% and 100% of it looks cut and pasted out of some HR database - usually the bullet points don't even look like they would go with the same job. Hell, sometimes they aren't even in the same font.

If that's how you're communicating to prospective teammates, how are they supposed to write anything back that's meaningful?

Or, let's say you ask for exactly what you're looking for:

a highly motivated team-player with a passion for doing a great job.

Then what would happen if you got a resume from someone that said "Hi, I'm a highly motivated team-player with a passion for doing a great job"? Would you put them at the top of the interview list?

I doubt it.

You'd probably shake your head and click delete, maybe grumbling something about poor communications.

What does all this circular, illogical behavior tell us?

When you get down to the heart of matter, resumes can't tell the story of being highly motivated, they can't prove that someone is a team player, and a resume can't make you think someone really loves doing a great job.

So what do we do instead?

We look for education and job title.

These two pieces of information are the lowest common denominator.

The bare minimum.

We want to believe that if a prospective teammate can get a degree in a field and work their way up to a cool title, that they must not be terrible.

I've got some more bad news for you.

People with degrees and titles can still be terrible.

Sometimes, people get a degree in a field through the academic process, but seem to have no worldly clue on how to use any of that knowledge in a real-life work setting.

I went to college with a guy who got all the test answers for every class from friends who'd taken the classes a few years earlier. He even had examples of all the essays to see how people did.

He got the same degree I did.

It doesn't stop in college, either. Sometimes, people get into a job and are promoted or moved into a position with a cool title and they end up being epic failures.

That last part usually doesn't show up on the resume, but you can bet that sweet title that they sucked at will be in there in big bold letters.

I've met tons of people who got a degree and a title that were terrible.

Haven't you?

If you're like most people, you've actually lost out on an opportunity to someone that was worse at the job than you would have been, but they got the role because they had a degree or a title that trumped yours.

But you still look at education and the most recent job title when you look over the resume, don't you?

The funny thing is, there are so many exceptions to the rule.

The best data engineer I ever worked with had a degree in philosophy.

One of the best infrastructure guys I ever worked with got his undergrad in dramatic arts.

But we play it safe, we look for education and title because it makes us feel like someone else vetted them. If a school gave them a degree, they must have some level of proficiency... we hope. If a big company gave them a title, it must mean they were good... we think.

No we don't. We're fooling ourselves if we think that's really true.

We do these things because the qualities we want can't easily be conveyed through text.

Resumes aren't the best medium for telling those stories, especially when they've been reduced to keyword-laden boilerplate aimed at getting through robot reviews.

So what can we do?

How can we rise above this nonsense?

For starters: read the actual resumes. They aren't the greatest way to convey these ideas, but it's the only thing you have at this stage.

Look through the accomplishments, comb through the words to see who might be a good fit. Sift through everything that is in there before weeding them out of the process.

More often than not, a "feel" for the top candidates comes out of resumes, not a checklist of items you're looking for.

If you want that to be a more fruitful endeavor, put a little effort into making a better job description instead of cut-and-pasting whatever garbage nonsense the last manager threw out there.

I can't tell you how many times I've had someone show me a job description and we just laugh because we can't figure out what it even means.

As I'm writing this, I wanted to see how vague some of this stuff is, so I went to LinkedIn and searched for "manager" to see what came up.

I'm not joking or making anything up. This is a real experiment I'm doing as I type the first draft of this book just to see what's out there.

I don't even know what a lot of the titles mean.

Do you have any idea what a New Verticals Manager is?

How about a WFM Transformation Manager?

Senior Program Manager - NonTechnical? They're literally telling me what the job *isn't!*

FMB Manager? I couldn't figure this one out until I went to UrbanDictionary (NSFW).

I found one for a CIAS Manager and even Google doesn't seem to know what that means.

There were actually six postings on the first page that just had a title of "Manager" - what the heck is anyone supposed to do with that?

Here's the description from one of them (a Fortune 10 company - yes 10, one of the biggest companies in the whole world):

"The Role: You are someone who is willing to roll up your sleeves. You are customer obsessed and thrive in a fast-paced environment while demonstrating the ability to deliver results. You demonstrate a strong work ethic, excellent ownership, the ability to meet deadlines and a willingness to learn new things."

Any idea what this job is?

Me neither.

Wanna take a gander at how likely it is that their perfect candidate applies?

I'm gonna guess it's not very likely considering no one even knows what that means.

What does the perfect resume even look like for something like that?

"Hi, I'm Bruce Wolf and I'm willing to roll up my sleeves. I'm customer obsessed and I thrive in fast-paced environments while demonstrating the ability to deliver results."

I feel like a tool just typing that. What if I majored in Customer Obsession with a minor in Sleeve-rolling, would that help?

That nonsense isn't gonna make it through the keyword machine, and if a human actually looks at it it, they're probably not going to bother reading it once they hit that line.

I know it's common practice to write resumes that basically just parrot back the job description (because so many companies just use terrible algorithms to select candidates), but this one is even more terrible than most.

Be specific in your job descriptions, not vague.

If I say I want a "Portfolio Manager," you might think I mean someone investing in stocks. What I really mean is I want someone to manage a portfolio of projects. And when you buy a copy of this book for your best friend (because it's such a great book and you're such an awesome friend that you didn't even wait for their birthday), they're gonna think I mean someone who managed an art gallery!

In this critical phase-one step to building a highly productive team, we've been trained to cut and paste terrible job descriptions and barely glance at the responses to get down to a pool of candidates.

Do better.

Separate yourself.

Write good job descriptions. Scratch that. Write *great* job descriptions. Explain exactly what you're looking for.

Then take the time to read through the resumes.

People took hours to craft each of those perfect paragraphs. That doesn't mean you owe them anything, but it is the best way you have at this point to see if they're actually the kind of person you want on your team.

So peek at the education and job title, but also read through the actual meat of the document to try to find the right candidates so you aren't wasting your time when you get to interviews.

3

WHY MOST INTERVIEWS ARE STUPID

Ok, so we defined what we're looking for in team members for a highly productive team (works well with others, motivated and driven, cares about doing a good job), and we've been through a great resume process to find the best candidates (because you didn't cut and paste a nonsense job description out there and let the keyword filter tell you which people to interview), and now we're ready to interview.

And what do we ask people?

"Tell me your biggest weakness."

Ludicrous.

This is not a good way to find out if this prospective teammate will help you have a highly productive team.

Managers really do this. They'll say they want someone driven who works well with others, then they'll cut and paste a terrible job description, glance at resumes for education and titles, and then get someone in a room and ask them what their biggest weakness is.

Then they'll complain that their team isn't highly productive.

Ugh.

Looking at this process holistically, it's easy to see where the big disconnects are. There's a total lack of continuity in the three major phases of building a team that seems to go unnoticed as we go through each step.

Why is this?

The deeper we go into the process, the more we do things that don't make sense.

If we want a highly productive team, we need to break out of the habits that make it so difficult to have a highly productive team.

Yes, it's that obvious.

In the interview state, we're finally past the barrier of a two-page, keyword-approved, digital document and we get to meet real-live people in person.

Now we can actually get to know these people, we can really delve into their unique skillets, experiences, and work styles to truly find out if these are the kind of people that can mesh seamlessly with our teammates and help foster a highly productive team.

And what do we say to them?

"What's your biggest weakness?"

"Where do you see yourself in five years?"

"Why should we hire you over the other candidates?"

Are you really going to get anything out of these answers?

Is there a weakness you *want* to bring on your team? Or are you going for the candidate that has no weaknesses? If you get someone that says they have no weaknesses, would you even believe them?

Do you care where this person sees themselves in five years? If this is a person going through interviews for a new job, I think it's a fair bet that they have no clue where they're going to be in five years. Is this supposed to judge their ambition? Do you want someone to join your team because they're ambitious, or do you not want them to join your team if they're not going to stay more than five years?

Why should you hire them over the other candidates? Come on, they don't even know who the other candidates are!

These questions are like asking someone if they're a liar.

The answer won't help you.

4

CONSIDERING TEAM IN INTERVIEWS

I f you want to get the most out of the interview process, think about what you really want out of this person.

Whatever the technical skills that are required, I know this: you want someone who makes your team better.

Right?

Brilliant, that's the kind of arcane secret wisdom you're reading this book for!

Now step back and look at the big picture. Think really hard about what will make your team better.

Think about it hard enough and there's a counter-intuitive truth that comes out of this stage of cultivating a highly productive team:

You don't want to hire the best person for the job, you want to hire the best person for the team.

This is hard.

There's so much to not like about this, especially if

you're in a logic-based mindset, but bear with me, let me give you an example.

I like sports, so I'm going to use a sports analogy.

Patrick Mahomes. I hope you're all familiar with him. NFL MVP and Super Bowl winning quarterback, one of the best players in the NFL. He has incredible arm strength, amazing accuracy, all the mental tools to read a defense, plus he's very mobile.

He's the total package.

But if I'm putting together a football team, and all I have is a roster full of Patrick Mahomeses, I'm gonna get smoked.

Why?

Because a football team needs a variety of skills.

You want a passer that can do all the things that Patrick Mahomes can do, but you also need people to block for him. You want big, strong guys who can keep the defenders at bay. It doesn't matter if they can throw, that's a totally different skill set.

A successful football team also needs some people to catch the ball. Patrick Mahomes needs someone to throw to, and the skill set for receivers is a lot different than the skill set for his blockers. Receivers have to be good at catching the ball, they need to be fast enough to run away from defenders. It doesn't make any difference if they can push defenders around.

Then on defense, you need guys who are good at tackling - it doesn't matter if they can catch.

This is how you make a well-rounded team.

Ok, maybe you're not into sports. Let's try another example.

Ever play Stratego?

Each piece has a different function. A bomb takes out all the pieces except the miner. The miner can disarm the bomb, but almost every other piece can take out the miner. The Marshall is the highest-ranking piece, so he can take out the miner and pretty much every other piece. But the spy can defeat the Marshall, even though all the other pieces can take out the spy.

When you put all the pieces together, Stratego gives you a well-rounded (and highly productive) team.

Never played Stratego?

Ok, I'll make this really simple.

What if you're going to play rock-paper-scissors and you have a rock and paper? Then you go through the interview process for your next team member and you find an *amazing* rock. It's such an awesome rock. It's so tempting to hire the rock because it's such a great rock - it's waaaay better than the rock you have now!

But that awesome rock won't really make your team better.

If you take that rock, you'll have two rocks and paper, which means when you go up against a well-rounded team of rock, scissors, and paper, you're going to lose. Every. Single. Time.

Here's another example that might hit closer to home for you. Let's say you have a software development project for a client. You need someone to write the front end, you need someone to manage the database, and you need someone to configure the infrastructure.

You may have one person who can fill all these roles, but those are different skills and a highly productive team needs people that can do all of those things. If you have a whole bunch of great front-end developers, it should weigh heavily into determining what skills you're looking for in the next person you bring in.

5

HOW I FAILED AT HIRING

L et me give you an example of how I learned this lesson the hard way.

Early in my career, I was a software developer. Big time geek. I was a hard-core coder, loved writing code. I was the kind of guy that would spend hours tweaking a perfectly acceptable algorithm because I wanted it to fire one one-thousandths of a second faster (I may also have a competitive streak so strong that it's unhealthy).

I would have managers tell me that it didn't matter and order me to stop.

So I'd stop.

For a few hours.

Then I'd go home and work on it some more, trimming that thousandth of a second off the run time and emailing it back to myself at work so I could sneak it in without anyone noticing.

That's how much I cared about my code.

I know, it sounds a little over the top, but my code was premium stuff - it earned me some pretty good reviews.

Because of those good reviews, I got some more responsibility. I got bigger coding assignments, I got asked to lead training, I even got the assignment to interview and hire our next team member.

At the time I thought that was awesome, but looking back with the benefit of hindsight, I see that decision for the epic blunder it was.

You know what's dumb? Giving someone additional responsibility based on totally unrelated achievements.

In this case, because I was a good coder, I was put in charge of hiring.

Bad idea.

Oh, you won a sandwich-eating contest? Cool, let's put you in charge of the air traffic control tower.

Don't do this.

Well, one of my old managers did (they were a good manager, it just wasn't their best moment) and we both learned a hard lesson.

Now, I'm a personable guy, so I managed to run some good interviews, I talked about code, asked everyone what their biggest weakness was, and then I made my choice.

Guess who I picked?

I hired Duke (not his real name) - the best coder of the bunch.

As a coder, I knew how important coding was, and they were great at coding, so I picked Duke.

That's right - of all the candidates in the pool, of all the people I interviewed, I picked the person most like me.

You know what that meant?

It meant every time there was coding to be done, Duke and I fought over who got to do it. Coding assignments that came into our team were gonna get done *right*!

But every time our team needed to put together a project plan or a budget estimate, Duke and I argued over who had to do it. It wallowed in the queue. We'd both kinda not really see it on the work roster and hope that someone else would take it.

In short, Duke and I didn't have complementary skills.

That's why you shouldn't hire the best person for the *job*. You should hire the best person for the *team*.

Duke was hands down, far and away, the best coder we could have got. But he didn't make the team any better because he didn't bring a complementary skill set.

He was the best person for the job, but not the best person for the team.

Jeff Bezos is one of the most successful businessmen of all time. When he's looking to hire a candidate, he always asks himself, "Will this person raise the average level of effectiveness of the group they're entering?" (https://www.themuse.com/advice/3-questions-amazons-ceo-asks-before-hiring-anyone)

You won't raise the average level of effectiveness of a group if you bring in someone who's the same as everyone else on the team. You need complementary skill sets.

So how can you build that?

Read on, my friend.

6

IDENTIFYING TEAM NEEDS

First, you have to understand your team. Learn about your team members, figure out their strengths, see what areas your team could use help in. There's lots of ways to do that.

The Myers-Briggs Type Indicator (MBTI) is a good guide that's stood the test of time. It's kind of a personality test. It won't tell you who to hire, but it will tell you if everyone on your team has similar approaches to work (and therefore similar strengths). The scoring in this indicator can tell you if you have all judgers and no perceivers, which would mean your team could be missing some perspective when they make decisions.

I'm also a big fan of CliftonStrengths (formerly known as StrengthsFinder). This assessment helps you discover which things your teammates (and, therefore, collectively, your team) are strongest in.

For example, my strengths are: Strategic, Visionary, Futuristic, Communicator, and Activator. That means that

I'm at my best thinking in the clouds (Strategic) and sorting through chaos to determine a course forward (Visionary) that will help a team reach their goals for the future (Futuristic). Then, I'm naturally skilled at helping others understand that vision (Communicator) and getting a team moving on bringing those ideas to fruition (Activator).

This has played out in my career, where I've found myself most successful in roles like Corporate Strategy, where my job is to take in a lot of random information and think about it until I come up with a plan (don't judge - thinking is work, too).

Some of my lowest scores were around Focus and Consistency. This means that repetitive precision tasks do not suit me. I would go absolutely bonkers trying to sit at a tool press repeating the same steps on an assembly line all day. Could I suck it up and soldier on? Sure, but it wouldn't be the best use of my skills (or my limited sanity) and I'd be hurting the team if I got an assignment like that, no matter how hard I tried.

These assessments don't tell you what people are good at or can or can't do, they tell you what they're naturally suited for and what their personality aligns them to.

When you can give people assignments that fit their natural disposition, an intrinsic motivation kicks in. They're invigorated and gain momentum in their work that they wouldn't otherwise have, making them more productive.

This means that in order to have a highly productive team, you need members who have different strengths so they can take on different tasks. This doesn't just make sense from a logical productivity standpoint; it also keeps them happy (which also increases productivity - more than most managers realize).

Using assessments like MBTI and CliftonStrengths can help you better understand where your team is strong and where they may lack representation. Once you have a better understanding of your team's deficiencies, you'll have a better understanding of what kind of candidate will be able to strengthen your team and make them more productive as a group.

7

DON'T FORGET SOFT SKILLS

There's a lot of other things that go into building a highly productive team besides just matching temperaments and strengths. It goes beyond technical skills, too.

When we talked about football teams and Stratego and rock-paper-scissors, we focused on technical skills.

But building a team by grabbing a bunch of people with complementary strengths and great technical skills isn't guaranteed to be highly productive, either.

Let's say you're putting together a small application development team.

You go out and get the best technical skills in the company. You nab the best front-end developer in the company, you hire a hotshot database admin who's fresh off the speaking circuit where she was talking about how she revolutionized databases at your top competitor, and then your VP tells you that you're going to get the best infrastructure engineer in the organization as soon as he wraps up his latest project next week.

Then, you look and see that they all have completely different and fully complementary MBTI and Clifton-Strengths results!

Oh, wow - a complementary all-star team like that couldn't possibly fail!

... right?

Wrong.

Teams like this fail all the time.

They're still missing something.

On top of technical skills and temperament profiles, you need everyone on your team to be a decent and reasonable human being.

What if your awesome front-end developer thinks your database admin is too full of herself? And the database admin thinks that your infrastructure engineer is stuck up. Oh, and the infrastructure engineer still thinks the database admin owes him an apology over what happened at the holiday party three years ago.

Now your all-star team is a disaster before the first meeting.

People skills matter.

I'm not talking about being a slimy smooth talker or having that cheesy, teeth-brightened, salesman smile. I mean, just being a good person that doesn't let petty things or back-door politics get in the way of doing great things.

If you have a well-rounded team of people with great technical abilities and complimentary skills, but they all hold grudges and don't get along, you're not gonna have a highly productive team.

8

A BETTER CASE STUDY IN HIRING

I 'd learned a lot from my early days when I hired someone who had all the technical skills I could dream of, but wasn't a good fit for the team. Now, I was managing a different team at a different company and I had an opening to fill.

I knew what I wanted out of our next team member, and I put a lot of effort into making a good job description (not the wretched jumble of nonsense buzzwords the last manager threw out there or the garbage description HR had). Then I posted it and waited for the applications to come in.

There was a fair amount of interest and a decent number of applicants. One internal employee - someone who hadn't even applied - reached out to me while the posting was up. She said, "I'm not really sure about this. I like what I'm doing, but this job sounded interesting and I just wanted to learn more."

I set up a meeting, and she peppered me with all kinds

of great questions about how the team worked together, about my management style, about the senior leadership in the area, about what people liked and didn't like about the team, and a whole bunch of other questions that had nothing to do with technical skills or temperament assessments.

This showed me a lot of things. First, it showed me that she had initiative simply by reaching out to learn about the position. More importantly, it showed me that she cared about being a part of a team. It wasn't fake or forced, either, it was natural, it was who she was - someone who knew how important it was for people to get along with each other to having a highly productive team.

A week later, the posting came down, and I had a meeting with HR to review all the applicants and their resumes. HR recommended that I interview every single person in the candidate pool... except her.

Why do you think they said that?

They said it was because she had less experience than anyone else and she was at a lower level.

That's right, HR looked at the most recent job title to filter the resumes!

I was a little miffed and when that happens, I (occasionally) can get (just a tiny, tiny bit) sarcastic.

"You don't want me to interview her because she's younger than everyone else and at a lower level?" I asked.

"Yes," HR said, looking befuddled as to how I could even question such a universally accepted truth.

"Ok," I said, calmly fighting back as many sarcastic profanities as I could. "I get where you're coming from. I mean, that would make a lot of sense... if I was looking for an old person with a cool title."

I paused, but they didn't say anything. They just made sour faces like they didn't realize how hilarious I was. Since they weren't saying anything, I continued. "But what I'm really looking for is someone to be a part of my team, to dive into tough situations and work through them with logical thought and a willingness to partner. I need someone who can adapt and learn new things, and I think she can be a great addition. I'm not sure that being old or having a cool title will help with that."

Now HR's sour faces degraded to more-than-slightly perturbed faces.

Rightfully so, but I'd made my point (albeit in a highly juvenile fashion that they should have grown accustomed to after working with me for so long).

I get where HR is coming from, though. They focused on title and age like so many other people do.

They relied on a very logical string of assumptions:

1. Older people have more experience.
2. If someone has done more things in the past, they will probably be better at things in the future (i.e., "practice makes perfect")
3. If someone gets promoted along the way, it probably means that they have a certain level of proficiency and are therefore a safer bet.

Does that sound right?
Sure, it sounds logical, but is it an infallible maxim?
Don't answer yet.

Think.

Think hard.

Think back throughout your career.

Have you ever worked with someone who had been with a company for like 30 years and no one - including you - had any idea how they'd lasted so long?

Have you ever seen someone get promoted and felt like they were in no way the best candidate for the promotion? Or have you ever seen someone get promoted and it didn't work out?

If you haven't, you're in a ginormous minority.

These things happen all the time.

Yes, experience and education are great things, but they aren't a great way to compare two candidates. If you were comparing laundry detergent or minivan tires, raw data like this might be the be-all, end-all answer, but it doesn't work that way when you're comparing people.

In fact, it rarely works out that way.

If you're using title or level as your indicator, it means you're taking someone else's word for it - you're trusting that whoever promoted that person (someone who is probably a complete stranger, whose skill in talent evaluation is a complete unknown to you) made the right call.

So here's what it comes down to: do you wanna just take someone else's word for it? Do you wanna base your hiring - the most critical part of cultivating a highly productive team - based on an assessment of someone you don't know that was done by someone else that you may know nothing about?

I didn't want to.

So when I faced a situation where HR was telling me

not to interview someone (a person that I already had a good impression of) because they didn't have a title, I disagreed.

After wrapping up my sarcastic comments with HR and finding some common ground, I put together my interview schedule and included her.

I went through all the interviews and she really stood out. She was great. She separated herself by talking about how she approached the work and what kind of ideas she had for the future. The rest of the candidates leaned on talking about things that didn't really matter. They talked about what they'd done in unrelated roles, about tasks with no transferable skills, they name-dropped VPs they knew, and told me all about how "trying too hard" and "caring too much" were their biggest weaknesses (even though I didn't ask).

She did none of those things.

So, after meeting everyone, this woman, who had a great interview, was my clear top choice.

I was sure of it.

But I'm smart enough to know that I'm not as smart as I always feel.

I didn't want to make a hiring mistake. I wanted to make absolutely sure that she would be a great fit for the team.

I thought back to the most productive team I'd ever been on and how it got to be that way. The amazing manager I had at the time knew the importance of good teamwork and how simply getting along was a key factor in highly productive teams.

One time when she was preparing to hire someone,

she went through the process and found her top candidate, then asked us to meet with them.

She didn't ask us to interview them, though. She didn't want us to ask them for "an example of a time" or what their biggest weakness was.

She just wanted us to take them to lunch.

She'd already interviewed the person and checked out their technical skills and previous experience. All she wanted us to do was hang out with them for an hour and see how we got along. And she didn't want to be there.

I didn't realize how brilliant this was until much later.

If you're a good manager that delegates work and trusts your team, you won't be around to referee every interaction your team members have with each other to make sure they're getting along. They'll need to do that by themselves.

Ever been on a team where a whole bunch of people got along, but there was just one person who didn't mesh with the group or was just plain a buzzkill?

I have and it sucks.

Team performance suffers when everyone can't be their whole, authentic self and easily get along with everyone in the course of doing their work. When a big part of the group is hitting on all cylinders, exploring new ideas and Johnny Killjoy shows up, momentum screeches to a halt. That momentum can take hours or days to recapture, if it ever comes back at all.

That doesn't lead to highly productive teams.

People who don't get along with the group can cast a long shadow of low productivity and funlessness. It stops the team from performing to their potential and prevents them from creating a highly productive environment.

It sounds cold and juvenile to look at "fitting in" as a job qualification, but let me be clear: I'm not talking about some middle school notion of "cool" or hiring the person who walks down the call with the best strut. I'm talking about people working well together.

You need people to work well together on a team if you want it to be highly productive.

Ever work on a highly productive team where nobody got along?

Didn't think so.

Neither did my mentor, who had us take candidates to lunch to see if they were a good fit.

She'd already fully vetted the candidate to make sure they had what she wanted. Now she wanted to know how we felt about them.

Not only did this lay the groundwork for a healthy working relationship and highly productive team, it made us all feel valued and important, like she trusted us and our opinions mattered.

That's priceless - that's the kind of trust that can't be built with superficial gestures or cute greeting cards with kittens and that Wane Gretzky quote.

Looking back, I realized that it also, subtly but implicitly, made us all feel accountable for the success of our new teammate.

There was no way we could watch this person fail, then come back in a couple months and say "sorry, boss, you made a mistake hiring this clown." No ma'am, we owned a piece of this person's success. We had to make sure the team continued to run smoothly (and be highly productive) after the new hire came on board.

It was a brilliant move by my favorite boss.

So I did the same thing.

I had everyone else on my team meet with my top candidate. That's five more people. Five more meetings. Sure, it took some extra time, but really, it didn't even add a week to the hiring schedule. A week may seem like a long time, especially in the heat of the process, but really, taking an extra month to be absolutely certain would have been worth it to make sure we were getting the right person. This is someone we wanted to be on the team for years or with the company for decades.

Hiring the wrong person is something you have to live with for a long time, and the impact of that decision in terms of lost productivity is immeasurable. Your team's impression (and the whole company's impression, honestly) of you as a talent evaluator and as a leader is negatively impacted long after you get that person off your team - if you ever do.

Do you want to rush through the hiring process to get done a few days early and end up making a mistake that forever brands you as "the manager who hired you-know-who"?

I didn't want those problems and gladly took the extra week to let my team all meet with my top candidate.

The team came back with universally positive reviews. I think they all felt good about being involved, it made them feel more confident in the hire, and, (maybe my favorite part) it, subtly but implicitly, it gave them some accountability to help make their new teammate successful.

I hired her.

She was fantastic.

She got along with everyone and contributed to a great work environment. She was actually the hire I am most proud of in my career because of how I approached it. It may have been a little unorthodox (it certainly didn't follow the safe steps that the HR manual laid out), but it worked.

9

DOING BETTER INTERVIEWS

Interviews are your big chance to really get to know the people that you're thinking of bringing onto your team.

It's critical to take the time to get a feel for team fit.

You can do what my mentor did and have people on the team take them out to lunch, but you can go even further, too.

Wouldn't it be great if, instead of just asking questions and going to lunch, you could truly see how someone will work with everyone else on your team?

Then do it!

Have them work with everyone else on your team.

Sure, you can't show them actual work assignments with confidential information, but you can find a 15 to 30 minute exercise and see how the candidate works with the team.

It doesn't have to be anything big or involved. Maybe put together a puzzle. Take out a couple pieces, add some extra pieces from a different puzzle. Don't tell anyone beforehand and then see how they react to those unforeseen circumstances with the team.

You could even have a candidate work on a team-building exercise with your group. Do something like the egg drop problem where the group gets a bag of random stuff and they have to build something that'll protect an egg from being dropped off a ladder.

Ratchet up the stress while you're at it. When the team's getting ready to start the activity, tell them they only have five minutes. Then sit in the corner with a timer and see how things go. Watch how they interact with team members and see how they react to pressure.

These exercises won't test technical skills (there's plenty of easy ways to do that), but it will tell you about soft skills and team fit, which are every bit as critical to a highly productive team.

This process can take a little more time, but "Good things take time" and "Rome wasn't built in a day" are sayings that lasted lifetimes for a reason.

"Work smarter not harder" is a great motto, but there's a lot to be said for putting in some hard work, too. When you put more time into something, your odds of success go up.

This even shows up in nature. Just look at gestation times of some creatures. It takes nine months to make a human baby, no matter how many people are working on it (though I'd recommend at least two). It only takes two months to make a dog, though. Heck, you can get a worm in two weeks, and a fruit fly only takes 24 hours!

Fruit flies come out as maggots, though. You don't

want to rush through assembling your team and end up with a bunch of maggots, do you? You don't want to cut corners and get a worm, either. You want people, great people - worms can't build skyscrapers and fly to the moon!

Nature doesn't rush these things and you shouldn't, either.

10

DON'T RUSH THE PROCESS

Building a highly productive team is easier said than done (really, though, is there anything that's ever easier done than said?).

When we break this down into key steps, the task can get less daunting. To build a highly productive team, you need to:

1. Clearly define what you want from people
2. Write job descriptions and seek resumes that highlight those things
3. Involve others on the team in the interview process
4. Hire for the team, not for the job, to build complementary skills and a cohesive team dynamic

This takes a little extra time.

It's worth it.

Don't rush the process.

The worst mistake you can make in cultivating a highly productive team is to bring in the wrong people. Remember, a team is just a group of people working towards a common goal - make sure you get the right people, even if it takes a little extra time.

PART II

MANAGING A HIGHLY PRODUCTIVE TEAM

11

START WITH FOCUS

Once you've built this team of amazing people with complementary skills who will all work well together, you have to manage them.

So what do you do?

Get a great group of people together and start driving 'em to get results?

This is where lots of organizations and lots of leaders go wrong - they focus too much on results.

Sure, I want results. You want results. Everyone wants results. But results are the cart, they aren't the horse.

If you focus too much on the results without paying any attention to what it takes to achieve them, not only will you fail to have a highly productive team, but your entire organization will fail.

People are what gets you results.

Not that new piece of productivity software from the sales guy with great teeth.

Not the latest management fad from the Big 4 consulting firms.

People.

Bringing a group of people together to achieve long-term results takes a lot of work even if you've done everything right in building the team.

If you need a task force to come together and quickly deal with an immediate crisis, that's a different story. Those situations are rare and the energy that comes from a group of capable, unfamiliar people rising to a short-term challenge is not sustainable in the long term.

12

FOCUS ON RELATIONSHIPS

I f you're building a highly productive team for the long haul, they'll need to get to know each other. They'll need time to coalesce, time to get to know and understand each other.

Foster this environment.

Prioritize this long-term need over the immediacy of the short-term issues. Value people over results because people will get the results.

Remember, a team is just a group of people. Managing a team means managing people. Managing people means managing relationships. So by the transitive property (which, in middle school, you swore you'd never need in real life), the only way to manage people is to build those relationships.

People think of professional relationships like they're different than personal relationships.

They're not.

They're just relationships with people and if you try to

border some off with imaginary boundaries and preconceived expectations because they're "professional" relationships, you'll be doing a disservice to the relationship, the person, and your team.

And you definitely won't have a highly productive team.

When I think of professional relationships, I always try to think about them as personal relationships. Personal relationships - relationships that people define as relationships with people you don't work with - are a lot harder.

If you work with someone you don't like, you can just avoid them around the office, you can switch jobs, or you just wander around until the end of the day and go home.

This is one of the ways people try to short-change professional relationships.

But you can't do that with personal relationships.

For example, if you're married, you have to go back to your spouse every night. If you try to wander around the house and avoid them, things are gonna get really awkward. You have to manage that relationship.

I'm married. My wife and I have five awesome kids.

That's right. Five kids.

You know what they say about people with five kids, right?

Lots of the S word.

grin

nods knowingly

If you're reading this and you have five kids, you know what I'm talking about.

That's right, I'm talking about the big S word: stress.

And you know that stress means a lot of the T word: therapy.

My wife and I have gone to our fair share of couples therapy. I think talking with a mediator like this is one of the keys to a healthy relationship, especially when the stress of kids is a part of the equation. There shouldn't be a stigma on therapy, it's something we can all use.

I remember the first time my wife and I went to therapy.

On the car ride there, I was thinking about all the things I wanted to talk about. I was thinking about all the things we needed to hash out. I was probably thinking about the same thing most people think about on their way to their first couples therapy session...

I was thinking about how right I was.

I was thinking about how much sense my perspective made, about how the real problem was that my wife - as sweet and beautiful as she is - just couldn't understand my point of view. Oh, if only she understood how right I was and how much sense I made, then, and only then, would our marriage be instantaneously transformed to the blissful ever after that I see in Norman Rockwell paintings and Hallmark Channel holiday movies.

I was thinking about how quickly our therapist could help her see my point of view and fix everything. I was thinking we could set a marriage counseling world record if this guy could show my wife how right I am in under five minutes. Heck, maybe we should order a pizza before we start because we should be home before the delivery guy can get our house.

Then we got there.

We talked. I listened.

After a couple minutes, I realized picking up pizza on the way home might be a better idea (I was still looking forward to pizza).

We talked some more. I listened some more.

Along the way, we certainly missed the mark for Guinness World Record for shortest marriage counseling. I was starting to think we should have had pizza *before* we came.

We talked even more. I listened even more.

The more we talked and the more I listened, the more I realized how little I understood her. Going even further, I realized how little I understood *myself*. Why did I snap at her for this? Why did I walk around complaining to myself about that?

We all have different personalities, we're all special snowflakes. There's a reason for that. Not only do we all have different experiences, but they all affect us in different ways.

Something that invoked pity in you, may invoke disgust in me. Something that makes you feel sorry for someone may make me think they're an idiot.

The same experiences affect us in different ways. This is what makes personalities.

Taking the time to talk through these things with someone else helped me understand this and understand myself better.

Something else that really helped me understand myself was a program derivative of RLF, the Regional Leadership Forum. This was a year-long leadership development program where you go offsite for a couple days every six weeks.

The program develops leaders, but it isn't focused on management skills or traditional business leadership training. It's about understanding people and understanding yourself so you can be a better person and therefore a better leader.

It gets deep. People get emotional, people cry. People have to face themselves. It's not easy, but it is impactful, even transformational.

I came out of this program understanding myself so much better than I would have ever imagined. It was life-changing for me.

I'm a really competitive person. I knew that before going into this program, I've always been really competitive. Who wouldn't want to be competitive? What kind of loser doesn't want to win at everything? It's how I'd always been and I figured everyone was just like that.

They weren't.

I was actually competitive to an unhealthy level.

One of the things I focused on in this program was trying to understand why I was like that. What life experiences had made me that way? Was I just genetically predisposed to being competitive?

The answer was not sitting there staring me in the face. I didn't just mull it over while I had a taco and then suddenly achieve enlightenment and understand everything about myself.

It took a long time to even start to understand that small piece of my personality. Even with a long series of very open and vulnerable discussions, it still took months of intense self-reflection before it clicked and I really began to understand why I was the way I was.

When I was growing up, I didn't have a stable family life. I moved around a lot, lived with a lot of different families, and by seventh grade, I'd gone to seven different schools.

As a young boy, you learn how young boys that age work, how they think. It's a pack mentality, it's like Lord of the Flies with lunchboxes (side note for millennials: Lord of the Flies was an old book that was also made into an old movie - it's like The Bachelorette crossed with the Hunger Games).

In my case, what I learned was that boys that age pick on two people: they pick on the smallest kid in the class and they pick on the new kid.

For most of my formative years, I was perpetually both.

My defense mechanism?

You guessed it: competition.

I felt like if I was smarter than them at every subject, they couldn't make fun of me. I felt like if I was better than them at every sport, they couldn't make fun of me.

I pushed myself to try to be the best at everything so that they couldn't make fun of me.

Turns out I was wrong about that (middle school boys apparently aren't as logical as I led myself to believe), but I'd discovered why I was the way I was.

When I grew up, hung out with (slightly) more mature people, and got a smoking hot wife, that competitive streak didn't just vanish - it was a part of me and it still impacted my life long after I needed it.

That was a huge breakthrough for me, a life-changing

epiphany of self-understanding. It felt like the first time I got glasses - everything was so clear!

It took me 38 years to figure out why I was so competitive and the only reason I even figured it out was because of an intense personal development program where I talked through this for hours and contemplated it for months.

If I hadn't done that, I probably still wouldn't know why I was so competitive. I'd still assume that's just the way I was.

I would still not understand myself.

So I took that new piece of self-awareness with me the next time I went to couple's therapy with my smoking hot wife. While I was in there, I realized that if I didn't understand myself, there was no way she could have a chance at understanding me. And if I didn't understand myself, how on earth could I ever understand her?

Then it dawned on me that she, too, is most likely cursed with the human condition and probably didn't fully understand herself, either - much like I didn't understand myself.

You probably don't understand yourself as much as you think you do, either.

Nobody understands anybody.

Not even themselves!

It's mind-blowingly complex.

That's what we're dealing with when we navigate the complexity of human relationships.

One person trying to connect with one person is really hard. Husbands and wives dedicate their lives to understanding each other, usually with mixed results (at best).

Trying to connect three or four or five people all with each other creates a web of exponentially more complex connections. When those people only see each other a few hours a day for maybe five days a week, just for the couple of years that they're on a team together, it gets even more difficult to foster a relationship.

That's what you as a leader have to navigate when trying to create a highly productive team. A web of convoluted relationships, made exponentially more difficult with each change in membership, with very limited time to sort through.

Yet, some people think that kind of relationship building doesn't matter.

They wave a dismissive hand and say "They're professionals, they'll figure it out."

No, they aren't professionals.

They're people.

They're people that you have to have a relationship with. If you want to maximize the productivity of your team, you need to foster those relationships.

Imagine you're having issues with your spouse (the most important working relationship you can have) and you say to them: "Be a professional, figure it out. Don't you know how to be a spouse?"

No.

I wouldn't like hearing that. My dear sweet angel of a wife certainly wouldn't like hearing that, either.

You wouldn't handle the most important relationship outside of work like that, so why would you handle the important relationships *at* work like that?

You shouldn't.

Not if you want a highly productive team. If you want a highly productive team, you need to build those relationships so people can work well together.

Building relationships is key to having the critical conversations that need to happen to have a highly productive team.

13

WHY BUILDING RELATIONSHIPS IS CRITICAL TO A HIGHLY PRODUCTIVE TEAM

Think of all the conversations you need to have on a team in order to be highly productive. You need to be honest with people even when it isn't easy. Sometimes you need to give unpopular orders. Inevitably you will come across a situation where you need to give helpful (though usually awkward) developmental feedback.

Those are hard conversations.

If you want to have a true, meaningful impact, you'll need to get to know people before you have to jump into those conversations with them. It's not easy to have hard conversations with strangers.

Think about it. Let's say you're sipping the earl gray of the month at some hipster tearoom, sitting down with your phone, checking out the latest kitten mittens video, and you hear a couple arguing from a table across the aisle.

You don't know these people, but their conversation is

getting pretty heated and then one of them says something really harsh, a low blow (too awful to even print in this book). You can see that the comment really hurt the other person, but the other person is arguing so much that they don't even realize they hurt them.

What are the odds that you're going to lean over, pull a complete stranger aside, and say "Hey, I heard what you said and I don't think you realize it, but that was a low blow - you really hurt that other person"?

The odds of that are zero.

Because that never happens.

I'm on social media (follow me on Twitter!), there's videos for everything that ever happens and there's never been one like that.

Strangers don't do that.

If they did, there would probably be a fight (and that would have *definitely* shown up on social media).

Now imagine you're out to dinner with your best friend, someone you've known since preschool, the person who stood up to your bully in 4th grade, the person who came to get you when you woke up in a cornfield with a splitting headache and no pants that one time in college. They make a comment to their spouse and you can see that it really hurt their spouse, but your friend doesn't realize it. When you and your friend go to the bathroom alone, you feel like you need to tell them.

Now, this isn't an easy conversation to have, but it's a lot easier than having it with a complete stranger in some hipster tearoom, right?

Why is it so much easier?

Because you've built a relationship with this person

over a long period of time. You know each other, you've been vulnerable, you've talked about things in the past. You've talked about difficult topics, even embarrassing topics. You've helped each other through tough times and built up an emotional bank account. You have comfort and candor and that makes it a lot easier to have difficult conversations.

And business is full of difficult conversations. Giving truly helpful development feedback, being honest about the value of certain ideas, telling him to never wear those suspenders with that belt again - if you want a highly productive team, you need to be able to have those difficult conversations.

14

CO-WORKERS ARE PEOPLE

You need to have difficult conversations to have a highly productive team.

Difficult conversations are a lot less difficult when you have a personal relationship with someone.

So how do you build that with people when you're stuck in cubeville with them all day long or some open-seating workspace with a guy who clips his toenails while he's on a conference call (and doesn't even mute himself so everyone keeps asking what that clicking is)?

There's a lot of ways to go about building those relationships, but I'm gonna cut right to the best, easiest way to do it.

Leave work early and go to the bar.

(Come on, you've been waiting for it, haven't you?)

Wait a minute, that sounds like something a big slacker would say! Did I write this whole book just to try to convince my boss that leaving work early and going to the bar is good for the team?

That's irrelevant. What matters is that you want to have a highly productive team and in order to do that, you have to build relationships.

So why not move a couple seats down from the toenail conference caller and just do it at work?

Because when you come to work, you're at work. Your brain knows it's at work and your brain has been trained by thousands of situations from other teams (that most likely weren't highly productive) to put up defenses when you walk into the office.

You don't tell off-color jokes (even when they're hilarious), you don't share everything about your personal life, you don't talk about that time in college when you woke up in a cornfield with no pants.

You put up barriers.

You make yourself a stranger.

This makes it difficult to build the relationships that you need to foster a highly productive team, but it's just the way people act when they get into the workplace.

The antidote?

Simple: get out of the workplace.

That's right, get out of the office and talk with your people in a close setting like a bar (or bakery or food court or any of the other options I mentioned earlier).

Team building events like going to Dave and Busters or a brewery tour are great - and necessary - but I'm talking about a more intimate setting. At Dave and Busters, you're there to play games (and drink). At a brewery tour, you're listening to someone else talk about hops (and drink).

These are good tools for building camaraderie

through common experiences, but they don't build the close, intimate relationships that can truly make difficult conversations easier.

Go somewhere where you can just talk (and drink).

Go to a bar or a coffee shop or whatever and just talk (and drink).

Now, I'm a fan of going to the bar. One reason is because I like to drink. Paired closely with that is the fact that one or two responsible adult beverages have a way of making people more likely to talk and share.

I freely acknowledge that this isn't for everyone

Some people don't want to drink for personal or religious reasons, some people don't mind drinking, but think it's not appropriate to do with coworkers. Some people won't drink when they go out, but don't mind if others drink.

Like so many other things, it comes down to knowing and understanding the people on your team.

So get to know them a little bit at work first. Feel them out for what types of environments they would be comfortable in outside of work and what you think might be the best setting.

Whatever you do, find the setting.

(If that setting does happen to be a bar, you obviously should not be going out and getting sloppy drunk and waking up in a cornfield with your coworkers. Save that for going out with your friends to the next county where your team will never see you)

Go to a bar, go to a coffee shop, go to a corner bakery, or a public workspace, or an ice cream parlor, or a hipster tearoom, whatever, just go somewhere you can talk.

Get out of the office and have a casual conversation.

Oh, but when?

That's always a great question (a great question that, not coincidentally, introverts ask to avoid social anxiety).

People are so busy at work that they always want to go out after work and have a happy hour.

Invariably, someone has to work late (or they say they're working late to make themselves look good, but they go home as soon as everyone goes to the bar... come on, you know you've thought about this).

Then there's always at least one person that needs to leave right after work for an important errand (which may or may not actually be real).

We know people are busy at work (or won't admit otherwise), but really, people are busy outside of work too.

I have five kids. I've got doctor appointments, dentist appointments, volleyball camp, swim lessons, soccer games, physics tutors, t-ball practice, plus we gotta eat - and that's just Monday!

Sure I'm busy at work, but I'm way busier outside of work. And other people are too. Even if they aren't, they'll say they are if they feel exhausted at the end of the day and just want to go home.

I've heard all the excuses.

So I tried something to make it easier to connect with my team.

I headed off all the excuses.

I made them leave work early and go to the bar (because I had previously talked with everyone and learned that they were all comfortable with a bar setting).

They were busy, but they were more than ready to go to the bar a couple hours early.

Every month or so, I took a few people from my team out towards the end of the day. We'd cut out at two or three o'clock and head to a bar and we'd just hang out and talk. I scheduled them like any other meeting except they were held at a bar instead of in a conference room.

I know what you're thinking.

You're worried about what people will say.

"That's a waste of time."

"Ummm... don't you have work to do?"

"Derp, the guy who wants highly productive teams leaves work early and goes to the bar?"

You're damn right I do!

Building strong relationships so you can work well together is the most important aspect of leadership.

You're not going to convince me that's not worth an hour or two a month.

An hour or two.

A month.

With all your garbage status reports and all your stupid meetings that could have been an email and all the time you spend waiting outside some executive's office because they're too important to stay on schedule, you really don't think that adds up to an hour or two a month?

Poppycock.

You spend more time late to work because of traffic accidents than an hour a month - that's two minutes per day!

Find that time.

Use that time.

Defend that time.

Protect that time.

This is important stuff and as a leader, you need to make sure it happens if you want to have a highly productive team.

If nothing else, it's a break. Everyone needs breaks. No one can go nonstop all the time. If you're working out, you need breaks between sets and your body needs rest days. If you're playing a sport, you need a break between periods.

It's the same for a mental endeavor as it is for a physical one.

But this is so much more than a break - this is one of the best things I ever did as a leader.

You'd be amazed at the things you can learn.

15

OH, THE THINGS YOU'LL LEARN

When you take your team out to the bar (or soda fountain), they'll tell you all sorts of interesting stories. You'll get to know them as human beings, you'll learn about their family, you'll learn about their childhood, you might even learn that some of your teammates have a wild side you wouldn't have guessed.

You'll learn all kinds of things that you never expected to learn.

I had a Moroccan on my team once. I'd seen Casablanca before, but that was about all I knew about Morocco. This guy taught me all sorts of cool cultural things (the interior decorating alone is fascinating), but the really important thing I learned about my Moroccan teammate was about his religion.

This guy was Muslim. I'd had Muslim friends before, even some pretty close ones, but there was still so much I didn't know.

I learned that Muslims pray five times a day. I knew they prayed a lot, but I didn't realize it was specifically five times.

I learned that their prayer times are on a schedule. Even though I'd scheduled things around prayers with my Muslim friends before, it never really dawned on me that they had a regimented schedule for prayer times.

I learned that the Muslim prayer schedule isn't dictated by a clock, but by the relative position of the sun as the seasons change and the earth tilts its axis (or, if you're a flat-earther it's just, you know, however you explain seasons). This makes sense because thousands of years ago, they didn't have apple watches and smartphone alarms to remind them, so their times were scheduled by the position of the sun.

That means that their prayer times shift about a minute every day.

I didn't know that.

Worse yet, their previous manager didn't know that.

Their previous manager did, however, notice that one day, apparently out of the blue, his Moroccan team member started showing up a little late to a regularly scheduled meeting. As the week went on, he just started showing up later and later.

Pretty soon he was showing up on time, then leaving in the middle of the meeting. After a while, he started showing up on time, but leaving early.

This manager, who didn't have good relationships with his team (and clearly never left work early to take them to the bar), never knew why.

He never asked why, either. He felt he shouldn't have to. He felt everyone should just "be a professional."

So he formed some bad opinions of his Moroccan teammate. He didn't have a relationship that allowed him to ask tough questions. He just figured his team member was kinda being a flake.

He wasn't being a flake.

He was practicing his religion.

I didn't learn about this until me and my Moroccan friend left work early and went to the bar.

This first-generation immigrant wasn't comfortable just joining a team and blurting out all sorts of details about his culture and faith, especially when he realized they weren't the predominant practices of the culture he was living in.

And once his manager formed a negative opinion of him (based on that manager's own ignorance and unwillingness to connect on a personal level), it made it even harder to open up and have that conversation, to explain something deeply personal that impacts his professional life.

Eventually, they did talk about it, but it was too late. Their relationship was already scarred and never really recovered.

In the end, he left the team - which was good news for me because he joined my team and was great.

I don't know if he would have been great on my team if we hadn't built a personal understanding, though.

I think a lot of people underperform because they don't have a good relationship with their manager. It makes things awkward when you need to have tough conversations. As a result, a lot of those tough (but necessary) conversations are avoided, then productivity suffers, which makes morale suffer, which makes productivity suffer even more.

It's a vicious cycle.

And the way to break that cycle is easy: leave work early and go to the bar!

Get to know your people, get to know about their lives and background, get to know about their cultures.

This story seems like a manager lost a great employee because he was culturally tone deaf. That's not the real point, though. The story actually had very little to do with cultural awareness, it was all about personal awareness.

Get to know people, culture is just one facet of that understanding.

I didn't just learn about this guy's culture when I went out with him. I didn't just learn about his religion and prayer schedule and how cool the sofas are in Moroccan living rooms (which gave my amazing, lovely, ravishing wife a ton of ideas on how to redecorate our basement). No! I learned about *him*!

I got to understand his childhood, his past work experiences, what sports he liked and what kind of books he read. I got to make a human connection. I learned who he was and as a result, we worked together so much better!

Please don't take an approach of "I got to know him *so that* we could work better together." That's fake. You can't force that. Just take the time to get to know them and the productivity will naturally come as you work better together because you have a relationship.

Get to know your team.

Even the ones you don't like.

Oh, I know, you love everyone, but be real, if you have a team of four people, there's definitely a fourth favorite.

Get to know them.

It's ok, you don't have to like everyone (trust me, you won't like everyone), but get to know them.

A lot of times, your team may be spread out across different offices or in different cities. That can make it a little harder to get that personal time, but it's still possible.

If you manage people in other cities, make time to get together, find a way. If it's close enough to drive, maybe you could meet halfway. You can have a full-day session at a central office where you talk strategy and work plans all day and have breaks in between to just have some one-on-one talks. Maybe even work all morning, then after lunch set up a series of one-on-one time slots for more casual relationship-building.

Have different people run the events to stimulate engagement - you'll get to know them even better when you see how they approach an assignment like setting up the event.

If that's not possible, use video conferencing to build a feeling of being there with someone. Heck, you can just go out to your car for a Facetime session with your remote people - whatever it takes to build a connection (that is, if Facetime is still around when you're reading this - otherwise just use whatever replaced Facetime).

However you do it, make it a priority to get to know the individuals on your team.

16

GROUPS HAVE FEELINGS TOO

Building a collection of one-on-one relationships is great, but it's only a part of the equation. To get a highly productive team, you also need to understand the relationship of the team as a whole. It's not just the sum of the parts, a group has its own unique personality separate from those of the individuals.

One of the worst mistakes a leader can make is saying "Hey, here's my leadership and management style" and then expect everyone to fall in line and work that way.

Sharing your style is a great start to the relationship, it comes from wanting to bridge that understanding, but it misses a huge part of the equation: the work style of everyone else on the team.

You can't have a highly productive team with a one-way relationship where the manager dictates how things will be based on their personal style preference. A leader who wants a highly productive team will need to understand how the team wants to be managed and build common understanding around the best way to work together.

A marriage wouldn't work if one of the partners came into the relationship saying "this is how I am" and just expected the other person to fall in line.

The same is true in work relationships, the relationship between a manager and a team.

Now *ahem* we make this easy by offering a facilitated service called leader assimilation (you can find it on our website because book royalties alone don't feed and clothe five kids), but you can use a skilled internal facilitator, too - just try to get someone as neutral as possible, someone with no personal or professional ties to your team.

Here's the general idea: A leader gets together with their entire team and a facilitator. They talk about the purpose of their team, their mission, their strategy, and all the things they want to accomplish together. This is surprisingly not as straightforward as it sounds - if you ask everyone on your team individually what they think the purpose of the team is, I'll wager the answers will differ a bit (if not - well done, you're in the top 10%).

After the purpose of the team is established and clearly understood by everyone, the leader leaves the room and takes time to write down questions they want to ask the team, questions like "how do you prefer to be managed" and "what do you expect from me as a leader" (in a facilitated session, we also provide sample questions to help out).

While the leader is busy with that, the facilitator works with the team to come up with their questions for the leader. They can ask the leader anything, like how they prefer to work or what they think is important from his team or just what their pet peeves are.

Then the leader comes back into the room and they exchange questions, taking the time to make sure everyone is clear on what is actually being asked. Once they're all clear, the leader goes out to another room to reflect on the questions and put together thoughtful answers.

During this phase, the leader usually ends up thinking about things they've never thought about before. Not only does this help them be a better leader by considering all these new questions, but they also get a better understanding of the personality of the team as a whole based on the questions they're asking.

At the same time, the facilitator leads the rest of the team through answering all the questions from the leader. This is a critical part of the process, where your facilitator really needs to be paying attention. There's usually a lot of different viewpoints and answers to these questions. The individuals all have different answers, but they need to answer as a team.

Once all the answers are defined, the leader comes back to the room and shares their answers with the team. Then the facilitator shares the team's answers with the leader - this is key because it can be really hard for people to share exactly how they feel about their boss - the facilitator is there to make that a smoother process and they can add their own insights as they observe the group.

In addition to getting to know everyone as individuals, this process allows you to also get to know them as a group to understand the best way everyone can work together.

When you know everyone on your team at a more personal level and you can hash out your work styles at a group level, it makes it a lot easier for the next step: connecting your team to the work.

17

CONNECT YOUR TEAM TO THE WORK

After all the time you've taken to get to know the individuals in your group and understand them as a team, the next step can be easy to gloss over.

Of course you're going to assign work and give everyone something to do, but in addition to handing out work, you also need to *connect* people to the work.

As a leader, you're in all kinds of meetings where priorities are churning like the sea in storm. You gotta try hard to keep up and remember that the executive committee took you from prioritizing sales incentives to focusing on marketing initiatives and back twice before settling on compliance as the top priority for the quarter... all before lunch.

Goals, objectives, and priorities change all the time. You're lucky to be in enough meetings to have insight on it, but explaining it all to your team and keeping them up to date on all the swings can be time consuming at best and nearly impossible at worst.

Some managers think they should tell their teams as little as possible, just giving them the high-level details. They say things like "they don't need to know that to do their job."

Maybe they don't *need* to know that to do their job, but knowing that will probably help them do their job better. Knowing that will probably help them be highly productive.

You don't have to give your team the blow by blow of every time an EVP overruled an SVP or describe the childish remarks they made about their pet projects (unless they're really funny), but keeping your team in the loop on the general shifts in focus (and why those happened) is critical to fostering a highly productive team.

Why?

Because people don't work well in a vacuum - they need context to do their best work.

Don't believe me?

What if I told you to wake up every morning, swish foul-tasting poison around in your mouth and then spit it out?

Don't ask questions, just do it!

That would be hard to follow, wouldn't it?

But if I explained that mouthwash can get between your teeth and kill otherwise unreachable germs that can cause tooth decay and gum disease, you might be more open to the practice, right?

Understanding context can have a big impact on

performance. Help your people understand context to connect them to the work.

If people don't feel connected to the work, they can't thrive, they can't contribute, and they can just fade away. They don't leave the team or the company, they just end up hanging out by the coffee machine a lot more, taking longer lunches, spending more time on their phones. They might even leave work early and go to the bar... but they'll do it alone.

Not connecting people to the work leads to a bad mindset.

If you're not gonna tell me what's going on, how can I do anything, anyway? Whatever I'm working on will probably change and I won't even know why.

Psh, I'm just gonna go on Snapchat instead (I hope that's still a thing by the time you're reading this).

I'm not pointing fingers, either. I see this in myself, sometimes. It's a natural reaction. If there's a lot going on with my manager and she's really busy and doesn't have time to talk to me and I don't know what's going on, I get frustrated. It's how I am, it's how we're all built to some degree. I feel like I can't do my best if I don't know what's going on. None of us can. When this happens, we get disengaged.

When people get disengaged, it's the first step in creating a toxic environment.

As a leader, it's your job to make sure this doesn't happen.

You have access to knowledge that your team doesn't.

Knowledge is power.

Sharing knowledge is sharing power.

Sharing power is the definition of the word empowerment!

If you want to get the most out of your team, give them all the information you can so they can be empowered and equipped to perform to their potential.

Having an attitude of "Well that doesn't concern you" or "You don't need to know" or "I'm too busy to talk right now" creates an information cartel. It's a huge barrier to building a healthy, engaged team. It prevents people from realizing their potential, and it destroys any possibility of a highly productive team.

Your team will be much more effective (and you will look like a much better leader) if you bring them up to speed - at least on a high-level - on all the things going on above them that they aren't directly involved in so they have the context for everything they're doing.

This is hard, especially when you don't sit next to each other or are in different cities, but you need to make it happen.

Find a way.

At the very least, take 10 or 15 minutes every week or two to debrief with your team on what's happened in the meetings you were in and let them ask questions. This is so easy to forget when you feel like a hamster with a Red Bull IV running on a wheel for ten hours a day and it's even easier to forget if you're not sitting next to each other.

As Ally Bubb writes in *Change Authentically - A Guide To Transform Your Job And Life Through Positive Action*: "It's way too easy to be caught up in the urgent and seemingly important minutiae of our daily lives and to blink and have a month, quarter, year, or even decade go by before we look up and wonder how we got where we are."

It's one of those things that can be out of sight and out of mind - you're in the know, so it's hard to remember that everyone else isn't.

Don't forget to take the time to share your knowledge every chance you get. It'll strengthen your relationship and it will make them more productive.

18

DRIVE ACCOUNTABILITY

Ok, so you've put together a great team, got to know them better as individuals, learned to understand them as a group, and you've got them connected to the work.

All you have left now is, you know, doing the work (notice we're three-quarters of the way through the book before we talk about the work - that's how managers of highly productive teams approach things).

When it's time to do the work, it's time to motivate people. Motivating people is really hard and doing it without coming across as cheesy (and totally losing your team) is a very difficult skill.

To motivate people and avoid the cheese, the most important thing you can do is be authentic. However you choose to motivate people, make sure you stay true to your personality. If you step out of character for this critical part of leading a team, everyone will think of you as a phony with artificially-whitened teeth and it'll be extremely difficult to recover.

In addition to being authentic, you need to understand more about how people work.

The article "Your Brain on Dopamine: The Science of Motivation" by Kevan Lee explains the basics very well (http://blog.idonethis.com/the-science-of-motivation-your-brain-on-dopamine/).

Lee focuses on the biology of dopamine, a chemical in our brain that makes us feel good. Dopamine pops into our head (literally) whenever you do anything pleasurable. That could mean eating delicious food, hearing a funny joke, or... anything else that you would define as pleasurable (no judging).

Lee has researched ways to use knowledge of our brain chemistry to increase motivation, which will make teams more productive. In his article, he lists three keys ways to leverage dopamine in motivation:

1. Record small accomplishments
2. Share results with your team
3. Stay on micro-deadlines

The second one (share results with your team) ties back to what we just talked about (you didn't think I'd cite an article that contradicted my point did you?). Sharing information is powerful.

The other two (record small accomplishments and stay on micro-deadlines) are focused on small time spans.

At work, we tend to focus more on big broad strategies

and goals so gigantic that they seem unattainable. Then the timelines always drag out.

You know how it is. Everything takes longer than planned. That project that needed to be done by the end of the year, just needs another month. And if it's going to go through January, it's probably fine if it wraps up by the end of Q1. Well, unless we need to push it back a little for other priorities. By then it's summer and everyone goes on vacation, then there's annual planning, pretty soon it's the holidays. Maybe it'll get done by the end of the year, but if not, it'll *definitely* finish in January.

Rinse and repeat.

A six month effort stretches to three damn years.

No biggie, right? After all, those key performance indicators only need to move a fraction of a percent each year (because they were made by executives who have bonuses riding on them).

Everything is long term, but here we have a scientist telling us to focus on small accomplishments on micro-deadlines.

Why is that?

Because we're built for it! We're built with small attention spans (especially me). We're biologically geared to do short-term tasks and the way our bodies dispense dopamine is just more evidence of that.

Get food, make babies, get sleep. This is what we're wired to do and none of those things are long-term endeavors (spare me your bragging).

Our bodies are conditioned for short-term motivation. This is why no one is cheering when that six-month effort stretches to three years.

On the flip side, this is why social media is so popular. These apps are built on tiny 280-character messages or a single picture with a caption, yet we get stuck on them for hours!

How?

Biology.

Each time we get through one of those tiny little messages, it makes us feel like we accomplished something. You read a two-sentence tweet. Yay, you finished something. So your brain gives you a little boost of dopamine.

That felt good.

So you read another one. More dopamine. Ooh, that felt good. So you read another one. Mmmm, nice. You read another one. And another one. Then your alarm goes off and you realize you didn't sleep all night.

Wouldn't it be great if we could do that at work?

Great news: we can!

We can trick our brains. We can record small accomplishments and set up micro-deadlines at the same time with one magical word: "standup."

Yeah, groan about it, I know.

You've heard it all before. Every productivity guru keeps talking about how standups are so great.

So then why does everyone at the office think they're a big waste of time?

Because they're doing them wrong!

How do I know this? Because I used to think they were a big waste of time because *I* used to do them wrong, too!

We set up all these stupid little meetings where everyone gets together and says "here's what I did yesterday." Then they come back the next day and say "here's what I did yesterday" and it sounds exactly like what they said at the last meeting.

After a few more rounds of people saying the same thing, they stop showing up.

Then the meetings get cancelled.

What a waste of time.

Why does this happen?

Because most of the things we do are big projects that span months or even years. Think about a huge project like road construction.

If you just say "I worked on the new interchange today," seven times in a row, of course it's going to get boring and seem stupid.

The key to making standups successful is to break the work down into smaller pieces.

Like Dr. Lee says "small accomplishments" and "micro-deadlines."

That doesn't mean breaking your four-year project plan down into 30-minute increments, it means that when you get together, you talk about the small things you did.

Ok, so you didn't finish the interchange, but did you complete a major phase? No? Did you get a contract signed? No? Did you talk about the contract? No? Did you schedule a call to talk about the contract? Yes? Well congratulations! It's a tiny achievement, no one's gonna plan a parade or build you a shrine, but you accomplished something!

Celebrate tiny achievements.

Telling people about that tiny achievement does two things.

First, it makes everyone feel like they need to come to the standup with something to say. This is where leaders may need to prod a little. People will say things like "I worked on the plans" - of course you did, we know that, but get more granular. What did you do on the plans? What small piece did you finish? What tiny piece did you make progress on?

The second thing this accomplishes is another small dopamine release. Oh sure, everybody talks about some tiny stupid thing they did and everyone claps and says yay.

It's so corny.

Maybe it is, but you know what?

It still triggers that dopamine release. Even if people don't like to admit it because their accomplishment *logically* seems small in the enormous scope of the major multi-year initiative, our bodies still react positively to it. That's how the human brain works. Even when we know we're being manipulated, it still works. It's biology, it's chemistry, and if we take advantage of it, it works wonders.

Imagine if you celebrated something with your team as often as you pulled up Instagram. I'm assuming you're reading this when Instagram is still a thing, but seriously, imagine if you celebrated something with your team as often as you pulled up Instagram. There'd be a lot of celebrating and it would be a lot more rewarding than looking at beach pics of that girl you couldn't stand in high school.

That dopamine release is powerful.

You know what else plays with the dopamine in our brain?

Crack.

You read that right.

Crack.

I'm not even joking.

Crack cocaine, one of the most addictive substances mankind has ever encountered, works by manipulating your dopamine receptors.

Doing standups and motivation the right way can also manipulate dopamine receptors.

Imagine if you could make work as addictive as crack!

You can, if you do it right!

Finally, there's one last thing that you as a leader can do at standups to enable a highly productive team and keep them accountable: remove obstacles.

If anyone on the team is having any problems, they should bring them up at the standup. As a leader, it's your job to help remove them. It's not just because you're a nice person or you're coddling them, though. There's a very practical purpose for doing this.

When people don't have any excuses, when there's nothing standing between them and their goals, they don't have any excuses. They're more accountable and they get a lot more done.

Getting things done is what makes a team highly productive.

So we've created a great team, built relationships, connected them to the work, and removed all their obstacles. Everything is running great, so we're done right?

Read on, dear friend, we're almost there.

PART III

MAINTAINING A HIGHLY PRODUCTIVE TEAM

19

KEEPING A HIGHLY PRODUCTIVE TEAM HIGHLY PRODUCTIVE

Congratulations, you've built a highly productive team and you're managing it like a great leader! Looks like your work here is done, right?

Sadly, no.

Now you have a new challenge: how do you make sure your highly productive team stays a highly productive team?

Like any other endeavor, you have to do routine maintenance.

When you buy a car, someone needs to change the oil. When you develop a piece of software, someone needs to install updates. When you put up a building, someone needs to clean the toilets.

Sometimes, maintaining a team can be a less appealing chore than any of those activities.

A team is just a group of people and odds are almost 100% that people will come and go on your team. These moves are part of the critical circle of life for a team and navigating them to ensure that the team remains a highly productive one is a deceptively tough challenge.

It seems like getting a team assembled and up to highly productive status would be the big challenge.

It is, but it's not the end of the job.

As people come and go, new personalities are coming in and the personality of the group as a whole is changing. In many ways, you're creating an entirely new team every time someone comes or goes.

That means you need to create new relationships and do more assimilation exercises - approach it like it's new every time.

Even if no one leaves or joins your team, you need to make sure everything you are doing stays fresh with the people you have.

You may find yourself in a season where no team members come or go for a long stretch. The org structure may stay the same and the work may stay the same, but people still change.

In "Cultivating a Healthy Marriage" (a really great talk on relationships that I highly recommend even if you aren't married), Kathy Keller says "Time marches on, you don't marry one woman or man, you marry many."

This isn't referring to America's incredible divorce rate, this is referring to the fact that people change over time. You learn new things, you think differently, your personality changes, your MBTI might even change. When you marry someone, they'll become a new person over and over again without any effort.

You can have the same people in the same jobs for a few years and the entire team dynamic can still undergo a wholesale transformation because individuals become different people over time.

This is why it's important to keep those personal relationships up. You can't just go to the bar a few times and say "Well, now I know everyone, we don't have to do that anymore."

The people on your team have lives outside the office. Their kids go away to college, their marriages fail, their parents die, their side businesses take off, they get new puppies, and all those things impact who they are and how they act.

If you're not keeping up with people after you get to know them, you might as well have not bothered getting to know them. Really, did you put all that energy into connecting with people to let it fade after a few months and return to form as one of the multitude of teams that just show up, go through the motions, and barely produce enough to not get fired? You could have saved yourself a lot of time by just waving a dismissive hand and proclaiming everyone should "be a professional."

If you do an assimilation activity with your full team, you can't just assume that nothing will ever change just because you have the same people on the team. Obviously it's a good idea to do another assimilation activity if you get a new leader or half the team turns over, but it's just as important to do one after a couple years of working with the same people because those same people will change.

They will have new perspectives; they will value different things. The dynamic of the team will change even if the names and faces stay the same.

I know because it happened to me.

I did an assimilation activity after taking over a new team. It was great, I learned a lot and got some great feedback on how to work with the team. Over time, we kept leaving work early to go to the bar, keeping up our relationships, and working together just fine.

Or so I thought.

There was some latent tension building below the surface. Nothing ground-breaking, but some hang ups that kept the team from being as productive as it possibly could be.

I just didn't realize it.

It had been years since our first assimilation activity and it was starting to feel like we were straying from some of the things we'd discussed. I reviewed the notes, which seemed incredibly helpful at that time, but didn't seem right any more.

So we ended up doing another assimilation activity. It was all the same people on the team, but now, years after our first activity, these same people wanted different things.

Their perspectives had changed. Life events altered their world view. Organizational changes outside of our team changed their outlook. Shifts in corporate strategy and company-wide priorities also had an impact on what they valued, how they worked, and what they wanted out of me as a leader.

Same names, same faces, but different people.

We change as individuals. We change as teams. Heck, we even change as generations.

Look at what Simon Sinek said about the millennials (kids born in the 90s) in his 2011 book, Start With Why:

"Millennials are unmanageable in corporations because they are impatient, lazy and entitled as a result of bad parenting, addiction to cell phones and Facebook depression."

Ouch, that's harsh. He's summing up an entire generation in one sweeping general statement.

He's giving a huge group - an entire generation in this case - a personality, because groups have personalities.

Here's some more quotes:

In her book Generation Me, Dr. Jean Twenge says "'Generation Me' are ... ambitious but also disengaged, narcissistic, distrustful, and anxious."

Time magazine had an article that said "they would rather hike in the Himalayas than climb a corporate ladder. They possess ... a monumental preoccupation with all the problems the previous generation will leave for them to fix..."

A study by doctors Robert Raskin and Calvin Hall titled A Narcissistic Personality Inventory found: "entitlement, arrogance, and self-absorption at all-time high for people in their 20s."

Each of these quotes sum up an entire generation.

But you wanna hear something funny?

That Simon Sinek quote was about millennials, kids born in the 90s.

Dr. Jean Twenge's book, Generation Me, was published in 2006 and was about children born in the 80s.

That Time Magazine article was from July 1990. It was written about people born in the 60s.

That Raskin and Hall study? That was published on October 11th, 1979 - it was about children born in the 50s.

Interesting, right?

People don't still use those sentiments to describe those generations.

People change.

Groups change.

You need to keep up with them or all the work you put into creating a highly productive team will quickly be for naught. It's like rebuilding the engine in your car and then never changing the oil. Without that renewal maintenance, everything falls apart.

20

DEALING WITH PROBLEMS

No matter how great of a job you do in building and managing a team, there will still be problems along the way.

At some point, you will need to deal with them.

A lot of times, managers will take a very business-like approach to addressing issues in order to deal with them quickly and try to keep the team highly productive.

Too many times, I've seen the self-styled super-manager step into a situation with a cape waving in the wind and proclaim the solution to the team's problems in a stern, commanding voice. After all, they're the manager for a reason and they believe that reason is because they know better than everyone below them!

It's a great way to build resentment, drive a wedge between people, and shove productivity downward.

Throughout this book, we've talked about what it means to have a highly productive team. One of the biggest keys is treating people like people, understanding them, and working with them like you have a relationship.

One of the biggest reasons why this is important is because it helps us have difficult conversations and deal with issues in a healthy manner.

Well this is where all that hard work pays off.

Having great relationships with your people doesn't make difficult conversations easy, but it does make them easier. It's always easier to have a tough talk with a friend than it is to have a tough talk with a complete stranger (or worse someone who resents you because they feel you don't understand them).

Take your time working through these issues. Address them in a direct manner. Don't jump to the solution halfway through the explanation you get from the first person.

Listen, absorb, understand their feelings, then get other perspectives from everyone else who was involved.

Any other approach will negatively impact productivity.

Don't listen to what people are saying? They'll feel unheard and think their opinions don't matter. Then they'll stop giving them - I mean, why bother? Then your team will severely underperform.

Don't take the time to absorb what they said and understand how they feel? Then they'll feel like the listening you did was just superficial and that you don't really care. Who wants to give it their all for a boss who doesn't care? Again, when this attitude comes in your team will severely underperform.

Don't get perspectives from everyone involved? Not

only will you be making your next decisions and taking action without the full story, you will make everyone that you *didn't* talk to feel like you are favoring everyone you *did* talk to. They'll feel like they don't matter, they'll stop trying, and you will not have a highly productive team.

If you try to take shortcuts in dealing with an internal problem or disagreement, people will sense it, they'll feel it, and you'll probably make a poor decision in addition to decreasing productivity by ticking people off.

Worst of all, when you do those things, you're creating problems even worse than the initial issue - you'll create the kind of problems you can't go back and fix.

If your windshield wiper isn't working, you either fix it now or later, but once it's taken care of, you can see out your windshield again.

But when you let a problem within your team slide, it gets a lot harder to fix. The negative feelings and resentment that people feel at not being heard, not being understood, or not being included when they think they should be, never fully go away.

Those feelings fossilize inside us and alter our views of people forever.

It's not as simple as just changing the windshield wiper and seeing clearly again like nothing ever happened.

People aren't windshield wipers.

21

WHEN A PROBLEM IS UNSOLVABLE

The biggest mistake you can make as a leader is hiring the wrong person for our team. The second biggest mistake you can make is keeping the wrong person on your team once they're there.

It's never easy to move on from someone, but if you want to have a highly productive team, you will need to do it at some point. Even if you make all the right hiring choices, the people you hire will change and the personalities of the group will change over time.

At some point, you're going to have to let someone go if you want a highly productive team.

When this happens, you need to be proactive. These things don't take care of themselves.

I've also learned this from experience.

The hard way, unfortunately.

I had a guy on my team who was just miserable. He didn't like the work we were doing, he wasn't happy on the team, he felt he was underpaid, he didn't like his clients, heck, he really didn't like much of anything at work.

Naturally, his productivity was low (which I hope would be obvious to you unless you just happened to open the book to this random page - pretty much everything in here is advice to help you avoid situations like this).

His clients were unhappy and his teammates weren't thrilled, either.

I handled it like the Bobs from Office Space. I figured things would just "work themselves out."

I knew there was a problem, but I figured if a guy was in a role where he hated everything and everybody and nobody liked him and he was miserable, that he would, you know, leave.

Nope.

What did he have to lose?

He had a job that paid the bills and gave him insurance. He had basically zero expectations because no one expected him to do anything (and boy did he deliver). On top of all that, there was the spite factor: I came to learn that he basically enjoyed making everyone else miserable (it's not that he was a terrible person, he just got sucked down into petty disagreements and let it get the better of him; misery loves company).

This situation kept going on.

I figured no one would want to put up with this all day at work for a whole month.

Wrong.

No way someone would want to go through a brutal

year-end evaluation and then be put on a life-draining developmental plan by HR for the better part of a year.

Wrong.

Surely, they wouldn't want to keep dealing with this painful work existence and let it draw out for over a year and a half.

Wrong.

Whoops, my bad.

Everyone else on the team was brought down mentally, emotionally, and performance-wise. They spent hours complaining to me about it and probably three times as long complaining to others about it. Not only were they not working during that time, they were distracted and frustrated when they were working.

That doesn't even take into account all the complaining and lost productivity on all the teams he was serving.

And the whole time, while productivity ground to all-time lows, I listened and nodded like an idiot, certain that this guy would leave on his own.

He didn't.

I killed productivity by not recognizing it and addressing it.

Don't make that mistake.

Eventually, he was re-org'd out of the department, but he left nothing but smoldering ash and unfinished reports in his wake. The team never fully recovered as we eventually all took new roles, drained by the entire experience.

There's a lot more wrong ways than right ways to handle these situations.

It was a tough lesson to learn.

But I learned.

Later in my career, I became much better at identifying problem employees (hint: they're the ones everyone complains to you about).

I've become more proactive. If someone was struggling with the work, I helped them (like really, proactively *helped* them) find a new position in the company. If someone didn't like where the company was going, I helped them find a job at a different company.

Sometimes, though, for a number of reasons, you just have to let someone go entirely.

It's not easy.

But it has to be done.

Maybe it's not even their fault, but you still have to do it. And when you do it, remember that your team is watching and whatever happens (and however it happens) will almost certainly get back to them. If they don't like the way you handled it, morale will drop and it'll take productivity down with it.

Face these tough situations head on.

Don't make it awkward. Don't make it combative.

Be forthright. Listen. Answer questions as truthfully as you can. Don't blame anything on anyone.

Handle it in a way where none of your other teammates would object to anything you said (because what you say *will* get back to them) and you'll be able to minimize any damage to morale and productivity.

It's also just the right way to handle things - you should always try to manage like a decent and reasonable human being.

Remember that your team is in a constant state of renewal.

22

FINAL WORDS

Productivity is an elusive goal.
It's fluid and fickle, difficult to define and even more difficult to create.

Productivity is more art than science, but there are some concrete things we can build our art from.

To have a productive team, focus on the three main phases: creating the team, managing the team, and maintaining the team.

At every step, you need to filter out the noise, the fads, the consultants, and the guy who grumbles about "being a professional." Focus your decisions first and foremost on which approach will make the team most productive.

A group of decent and reasonable human beings who have decent technical skills can accomplish pretty much anything.

Build that team and manage it in a way that helps them maximize their productivity.

And once you hit that peak and feel like your group is

as productive as they can possibly be, push for a new peak.

Keep doing the things that got you there. The things we discussed in this book aren't trendy tips or flavor-of-the-month approaches - these are foundational core principles that will help you build a team dynamic that will never go out of style.

Good luck.

BOOK BRUCE!

Help the leaders at your organization foster high performing teams!

Bruce Wolf, who's delighted audiences on six continents, speaks to organizations like yours!

He's learned a lifetime of lessons from organizations ranging from Fortune 50 and Private 100 to dot coms and startups. He's worked for global niche leaders and regional chains as well as small businesses and franchisees. He's worked in financial services, marketing, manufacturing, retail, publishing, technology, volunteer, secular, education, and more.

Along the way, no matter the size, location, or industry a company is in, he's seen leaders make the same mistakes over and over again - he's seen enough to become an expert on how to ruin your company.

That's why he started HowToRuinYourCompany.com - his talks help leaders avoid the mistakes everyone else is making!

For inquiries about speaking engagements (including keynotes, panel moderation, emceeing, and more), contact: Bookings@HowToRuinYourCompany.com.

For more information, see http://www. HowToRuinYourCompany.com.

SIGN UP FOR OUR MAILING LIST!

Did you find this book interesting? Do you like the idea of leaving work early and going to the bar?

Want to learn more about other books when they come out, new talks on similar topics, and generally interesting stuff?

Our mailing list might be right for you...

Do you also want to be a part of a mailing list that will *never* (*ever*) sell your email or spam you every other day with nonsense (trust me, we hate that stuff, too)?

Then, our mailing list *is* right for you!

Sign up at:

HowToRuinYourCompany.com/NewsletterSignup

ABOUT THE AUTHOR

A technologist and strategist, Bruce Wolf has built his career at some of the most recognizable companies in the world.

Working for organizations ranging from Fortune 50 and Private 100 to dot coms and startups, from global niche leaders and regional chains to small businesses and franchisees, in industries including financial services, marketing, manufacturing, retail, publishing, technology, volunteer, secular, education, and more, have taught him a lot about business, leadership, and about people in general.

He learned that no matter the size, location, or industry a company is in, he's seen leaders make the same mistakes over and over again - it's been enough material to become an expert on how to ruin your company.

That's why he started HowToRuinYourCompany.com - his talks help leaders avoid the mistakes everyone else is making!

He shares his lessons through his books as well as through his speaking engagements and unique leadership workshops, which have entertained and educated business leaders on six continents.

He also likes to swap business stories and connect with people. You can drop him a line at: Bruce@HowTo-RuinYourCompany.com.

THANK YOU

Thank you for reading - I truly hope you enjoyed it!

Did you like it?

Don't lie, high performing teams are only built through honesty. If you didn't like it, that's ok - you can just skip this page.

But if you really liked it, would you please consider leaving a 5-star review?

Reviews are the lifeblood of any book. Your review can help others find this book, in addition supporting me. Then you can go to the bar.

Thank you so much,

-Bruce

www.ingramcontent.com/pod-product-compliance
Lightning Source LLC
Chambersburg PA
CBHW060044210326
41520CB00009B/1258